MUSINGS

•

Poems by Vishwanath

Musings

Poems by Vishwanath

Foreword
Khushwant Singh

rajpal

1912-2012
100
Years of
Excellence in Publishing
rajpal

Price : ₹ 200/- (Rs. Two Hundred)

ISBN : 978-81-7028-946-3
MUSINGS (Poems) by Vishwanath
Printed at G.H. Prints Pvt. Ltd., Delhi

RAJPAL & SONS

Kashmere Gate, Delhi-110 006
website : www.rajpalpublishing.com
e-mail : sales@rajpalpublishing.com

Foreword

There comes a time in most thinking people's lives when they begin to ask themselves about the meaning and purpose of their existence. Who am I ? What was the reason of my existence? What will happen to me after I die? Adi Shankara posed the same questions to himself :

Kohum? Kastwam? Kuto ayaetaa?
Ko mey Janani? Ko mey taataa?

Who am I ? Where did I come from? Where will I go? Who are my real father and mother? Adi Shankara did not give any answers to these questions for the simple reason that no one knows the answers. All that has been written and said about the origin of life is in the realm of conjecture.

All that is said about what happens after death is likewise in the realm of fantasy, be it the Day of Judgement or rebirth in another form. No rational human being accepts them because they do not stand the test of reason.

I am not surprised that my friend Vishwanath, now in the 91st year of his life and with much achieved should ask himself these very questions and put his posers for answers into lyrical prose and verse. He begins in somewhat in the same tone as Adi Shankara :

Who am I ?
Why this mask on my face?
Let the real me stand up?
And face me.
But would I be able to face him?

Having questioned his own existence, the poet goes on to problems of the ego, his loneliness among milling crowds, his closeness to his mother and his partner in life. It appears that pent up emotions burst the bounds behind which they had been contained for nine decades and now flow unchecked. Other emotions also find expression : watching a turbulent sea with wave after wave crashing on the shore, a winter's day in the mountains with snow-flakes covering the landscape. And much else.

The collection is designed for private circulation; it should be made accessible to the public.

Khushwant Singh

Preface

I have no pretensions of being a poet. I had never thought of dabbling in poetry at any time, though poetry has been my life-long passion.

It was only during the past few years that poetry happened to me. It was like the bursting of unexpected rains, like a downpour of late monsoon. I penned a large number of poems in English and Hindi during this period.

Let me confess that my mind is hyper active and it operates at more than one level most of the time. It questions everything, it reacts, it reflects on every happening. This is perhaps the genesis of these poems.

This is a selection of my poems—good, bad or indifferent. I owe no apology for these. I only wish that you may find time to browse through them. Perhaps you may like or identify with some of these poems.

5, Racquet Court Road,
Civil Lines, Delhi-110054

Vishwanath
April, 2012

Contents

To
Sudhir, Kapil & Meera
for their love for literature

Who am I
Why this mask on my face
Let the real me stand up
and face me
But would I be able to face him

It is strange
But it is true.
To myself
I am a stranger

We have lived together
So long
We have walked together
So long
Yet, we do not relate
We are not intimate

If sounds strange
But it is true
To myself
I remain a stranger

Within me
A tempest is raging
A volcano simmering
A wild animal crouching
Sharp thorny bushes growing
all around

There is a deep dark jungle
within me

This day
I have taken off
all my clothes
one by one
and hung them
on the wall

Alongwith I have also
hung up
all my desires
my dreams
my aspirations
and
all my ambitions
and also
my name and address

I have a puppet
which moves and acts
smiles and frets
prances and dances
at the touch of my fingers

Now, however, it is not so
On its own
it moves to and fro
shaking his head for 'yes' or 'no'
putting on an act
and knows how to react

Am I the puppeteer
or the puppet

I am in a prison
It has no high walls
No security guards
No jailor
No iron bars
to bar my escape

Still I cannot walk out
I am confined
in the solitary cell
of my own self

A haze all around
It is getting dense
It has settled on the city
It has also settled
on my soul

I have shut tight
all the doors and windows
of my mind
lest the dark desires
whose entry I have banned
find their way
within me

Like a thief
who knows the art of sneaking
into even a well-guarded house
such desires do barge in
once in a while

I am getting smaller over the years
Earlier my creed
was the Vedic Mantra
VASUDHEVA KUTUMBKAM
'वसुधैव कुटुम्बकम्'
The entire world is my family

Now it is KUTUMBKAM
'कुटुम्बकम्'
Only my family

I am in a crowd
People jostle me
I am pushed around
I lose my way
I go astray

It is the crowd that is walking
Not I

A single leaf
weather-beaten
And turned pale
by heat and gale
dangles precariously
from a tiny twig

It is looking wistfully
down below
at the fallen leaves
and
is clinging desperately
to the tiny twig
for its very
life

A tear-drop
is a crystal ball
You gaze through it
you will see
the story of a lifetime's grief
writ in it

I cannot appreciate
a bonsai

It is heartless to
trim the roots and branches
every other day
not to let nature grow
to its
full splendour

It is as heartless
as to be amused
looking at a dwarf

My little girl
my sweet doll
plays with teddy bears
prancing around us all

I go for a nap
when I wake up
my little girl
has grown as
tall as I am

I am a child once again

My dear mother
washing my face
scrubbing my dirty hands and feet
combing my hair
dressing me smart
in a new shirt and shorts
giving a peck on my cheek
A pat on my back
And, pushing me out
saying
Now go and play

Life is like
a piano
It has
black and white keys
one has to play both skilfully
to create a
symphony

At times, my mind turns a truant
It escapes from its abode
to roam about shamelessly
on the forbidden road

It derives pleasure
in no small measure
from things which I detest

This truant
tho' my soul-mate
is the one whom I hate
It is like carrying a cross
an albatross
around my neck

The Earth moves
The Sun moves
The rivers move
There are moving scenes
Moving plays
Moving songs
But, the heart seldom moves

It is a traffic jam
my vehicle is stuck
not moving an inch
Still I am
honking the horn

Man is a river
shallow at places
treacherously slippery and deep at others
with subterranean currents
unfathomed

But, deceptively calm and cool
at surface

He is a fugitive on the run

He is a fugitive from life
He is a fugitive from himself
being chased by himself
He is the hunted
he is the hunter too

The fugitive is still in the race
of hide and seek
and chase

There's a cactus growing within me
It is sprawling all around
pushing at the four walls of my being
leaving little space
for me to breathe

I crave for the fresh breeze to blow in
to seep within the recesses of my heart
I crave for open spaces within
my being
I cry for freedom

I speak to please others
I dress to impress others
I make moves to move others
I look as others would like me to look
I look for their
approbation

I exist for others
I am no longer Me

The Sun emerges
majestically
from the East
in full resplendence

It strides across the skies
radiating the warmth of life
all over the Earth all day long

And, having done
its daily chore
glides gracefully
into the sea
to get refreshed and rejuvenated
to rise again

A pigeon and a dove
Are madly in love

They descend at dawn
at my small lawn
to partake of grains
laid out for them

Then the courtship begins
their necks puffed up
their love waltz begins
they move in circles
going round and round
emitting a love sound
'Guturgoo, guturgoo'
'I love you, I love you' →

and the one
is chasing the other
as if in a race
And then suddenly
they relax their pace

It is now time
to kiss good-bye
and fly off to the sky

Beautiful artificial flowers
in colourful hues and shades
in vases of jade

Statuettes of Buddha and Gandhi
in plaster of Paris

Furnishings in
look-alike jamavars

Replicas of Husain and Picasso
adorning drawing rooms

It is a
world of
fakes and make-believes

I am a Hindu
I was born so
Hindu name was stamped on me
which I carry with pride
All other religions I deride
I wear a saffron mask

May be in my next birth
I am born a Muslim
I may even turn a Jihadi
ready to kill kafirs
A green mask would settle on my face

I have no face of my own
I am a Mask

It is being said
Action leads to reaction
And, it is natural

So, violence would lead to
more violence
Bloodshed to more bloodshed
Arson to more arson
Murder to many more murders
Rape to more rapes

What a mind
to justify genocide

Dance of the Eunuchs

Eunuchs are coming
They come clapping, singing
And dancing

Eunuchs have
Their own
Communication network
They come to know
The when and where
Of any celebration

They have
A sense of timing also
When to make
Their appearance
And when to disappear →

They are adept at
Cajoling and coercing
And even blackmailing

Your praise
They would sing sky-high
If they get their
Pound of flesh

If you are miserly
They would sing
With a sting

Eunuchs are here
In our midst also
They also clap
And sing and dance
They also cajole, coax
And, even blackmail
To get their
Pound of flesh

My car stops at the signal
There is a rap at the window pane
I cast a cursory glance
A young girl
In a tattered frock
unbathed, unwashed
hair dishevelled
hand outstretched
A picture of
young innocence seeking succour

I look at her face for a while
The car moves on suddenly
That young girl
with her outstretched hand
under the scorching Sun →

Now just a fleeting image
like the lamp-post, the tree
or, like the news item
in the paper I was reading—
20 more massacred in Gujarat
10 jawans killed in Sopore
Figures and numbers
and no more

For the poor little girl
with her outstretched hand
I have not even sighed
For the countless dead
I have not cried

I live in a city
where souls are in deep slumber
And people mere numbers.

Liliputs are a happy lot
They sing, they dance, they make merry
In their own little world
They have a small kingdom of their own

They dared to make
the big and burly Gulliver, the globe-trotter,
their prisoner, as he strayed
into their kingdom
and dragged him to the city-center
to make him feel small—a Lilliput

Hurrah for the Lilliputs!

Our sweeper lady
brought along her three-year old daughter
so chubby, cheerful
and sweet looking
in no way less than
our own Convent-school-going
grand-daughter of her age

While her mother worked
she started playing with
the spare broom
trying to sweep the floor
like her mother

The telephone bell rang

"Yaar, it is long since we met
come over for a chat
I know my house is a long distance
I am not keeping well
you have to come"

I spontaneously said
Yes, I will be seeing you
in a day or so

After a month
again the telephone rings
"I know you are a busy man
you could not come
send me a few books to read →

I feel quite lonely
since my wife's demise"

I again said
Yes, I will be seeing you
in a day or so
and bring the books along too

After a week or so
the telephone rings again
this time it is not his familiar friendly voice
just a message
that my friend was no more
He had passed away in sleep at night

Since then
I am carrying the cross
of my unkept promise
to my dear departed friend
of college days

On the sudden demise of my dear friend, Balraj B.

There are two women
whom I love, respect and adore
One of course
is my dear departed mother
a picture of divine grace
with an angelic face
Who gave me the gift of life
And nursed me
with her toil and tears
thru' the difficult years
She is the one
who groomed me
into the man that I am

The other woman in my life
Is my wife →

A demure, petite girl
when into my life she came
turned out to be a woman of steel
in her frail frame
She has stood by me
thru' struggles and strife
thru' thick and thin
and
With her overflowing love
kept happy
my kith and kin

When I was
looking for a place under the Sun
after the '47 partition
She single-handedly
was steering the family
to its present position
And now she is the deity
of our small clan
over which she presides
with dignity and elan.

When lips
tenderly touch the flute
And
Heart pours out its very breath
into it
only then
Melody is born

Bad coins push out
Good ones
Thus goes the Gresham's law
It is the same with people
Good guys are given the boot
Bad ones rule the roost

Mundane matters
Casual chores
Always score

Prime issues
Live concerns
Keep languishing
As before.

What an impressive body
strong and sinewy
which others envy

What a sharp mind
No problem is too complex
for him to
mastermind

Alas
He has feet of clay
which under pressure
easily give way

Black spots
keep floating before my eyes
Opthalomologist says
It's nothing to worry
It's a common occurrence
that happens with age

I however wonder
whether these be
the blind-spots of my life
which have caught up
with age

The laughing Buddha
With his benign bulging belly
And an amused look
Sits pretty in my drawing room

He is laughing
At the goings on
Without any reason
Or rhyme
All the time

An ant
pushing a load
much bigger than herself
stops for a while
to say 'hello' to another ant
coming from the opposite direction
and after a while
continues trudging on with her load
as before

Now

We do not laugh heartily any more
We do not cry unabashedly
We do not talk freely
We do not sing with abandon
We do not love madly

Even with friends we are formal
Rarely normal

A rudderless boat
has no direction
It just drifts

Life without a purpose
merely breathes
just exists

'To be or not to be'
the vexed question
haunts me quite often

'Whether 'tis nobler in the mind
to suffer
or to take arms against the sea of troubles'
Whether discretion really is
the better part of valour
Whether to go for tact or truth
'These concerns make cowards of us all'

These concerns
often find me standing bewildered
on the crossroads of life

Quotes are from Shakespeare's Hamlet

Siberian cranes
from far away lands
flying over hills and dales
come to my beloved country
every year
in search of a sanctuary
in the cold winter

Like these silvery birds
my mind wanders too
to mountains and jungles
and holy rivers
in search of
a sanctuary for my soul

My old school friend
with his receding grey hair
and twinkling eyes
is with me again

It is almost a year
since he was here
He is surprised
to find that I looked just the same
only some extra furrows on my brow
a few more steaks of grey in my hair

He gives me a sharp gaze
to find out
if there were any other ravages of age
and bursts out in a hearty laugh →

saying
Yaar, you are as stubborn as I am
You are still at the steering wheel
merrily driving your 1920 vintage car

And with these words
at my back he gives a friendly slap
Saying, see you next year, Old Chap!

Every other person
in this wide world
is like Dr. Jekyll and Mr. Hyde
He waits
for the darkness to descend
to put on
the mask of Mr. Hyde on his face
to stalk the shadowy alleys
for his fiendish acts
And
as the dawn approaches
he is back home
to be the same
gentle and genial
civil and courteous
familiar and friendly
Dr. Jekyll

A tortoise
like a hunchback
is an unseemly sight

It can withstand
the lashes of time on its back
solid like a rock

It moves at a snail's pace
but can cover up to
fifty miles
at its slow pace
Truly, slow and steady
wins the race

My Mother

A picture of grace
an angelic face
yet, tough and tenacious
in times of crisis
She lost her valiant husband
in the prime of youth
She never let her children
feel the absence of a father
She had stepped into the role of our
father as well
Whether it was school fee
or pocket money
or extra expenses on summer excursions
She would
juggle out money from
her meagre savings →

without a hint to us
how difficult
the balancing act was

We never felt the pinch of paucity
We could keep our head high
with the more privileged classmates

How did she do it
She was totally uninitiated
in the ways of the world
or business affairs
which she had to take
under her wings
and, even here
she acquitted herself well

It was her indomitable iron will
tempered by her rustic roots
and abiding faith
which made her fill the bill
so well

For years
I have been
struggling to steer clear of the
quagmire called the world

Call it my luck
The more I try
to disentangle
the deeper I get stuck

It started with
a drizzle
Now it is raining
in torrents
Sharp winds
swaying the sheets of falling rain

Arms stretched out
head tilted back
I stand in the open
to let the rain fall
straight on my face

I want rains to seep deep
Into my parched being

There is too much
of 'I' in me
I do, I believe
I act, I achieve
I stop, I go
I say 'yes', I say 'no'
It is my gain, it is my loss
I am the boss

Why all this hullabaloo
about the bloated 'I'
which in reality
is a small fry

It was in New York
It was at midnight
As we came out of
The Concert Hall
The entire landscape
Stood transformed
Into a fairyland
As if by a magic wand
Flakes of snow
Were fluttering down
In an incessant flow
Like tiny bits of fluffy cotton

Snow flakes were gliding gently
To settle on our overalls
And, that was our
First feel of snowfall

Today I decided to have a straight talk with Myself

I made him sit beside me on a park bench
I said,
You have been a
hard task-master
all thru' my life
I am now tired
I am like the setting Sun
Why don't you let me alone
To do what I wish

He said
You are still fit and fine
First do the unfinished tasks
Heaped on your table →

I said,
Tasks are like Hydra's heads
As I finish one, two others pop up

He said
Now be quiet
We have come for a walk
Now no more talk

I dream of
walking barefoot on the oceans

Of flying like an eagle
over hills and dales

Of erasing pain and poverty
with a sleight of my hand

Of leading the poor children
to a land of smiles and laughter

Big dreams, these may seem
But, I am alive
as long as I dream

We are all merchants
seeking
our pond of flesh
from others
unconcerned
and insensitive
to their plight
like Shakespeare's
Merchant of Venice

. The train is
puffing and pushing
through a tunnel
long and dark
to find light
at the end of it

Who is he
within me
who does not let me be

Whatever I do
Whatever I say
Whatever I think
Whatever I believe
He questions all there
He would not
let me be in peace

He is indeed
an integral part of me
Even if I wish
he would not go
I wonder
Whether he is a friend or foe

Today the sea is in a rage
Like the roaring lion in a cage
Mighty, menacing waves
Are surging forward
Raising ten-feet high
Moving walls of water
Sweeping aside, tearing asunder
Whatever comes their way

But, even the mightiest
Meet their nemesis
As the waves reach by the shore
They recede meakishly
Leaving behind
A rail of froth and foam

I am scared
of the mirror
Whenever I look into it
A weird face stares back at me

At times it wears a sinister smile
And mocks at me
Flaunting a certain intimacy with me

I believe it is not me
I cannot make out
Who is he

If I do not move fast
I will be left behind

I cannot move fast
I cannot push myself in the race
beyond my placid pace

If I look ahead
I am the last in the line
But, if I look backwards
the first place in the row is mine

Let me live
the winter of my life
with as much warmth
as the summer of my youth

If youth was
Life's golden phase
Let my Sunset Years
be full of love and grace

Autumn leaves
of different huse
pale yellow, copper brown
rust and red
fluttering down
in a gentle waltz
to lay a carpet
of dried leaves

Dry, crips autumn leaves
Trampled and mingled with dust
whisper the ultimate secret of life

Dust thou art
and unto dust shall thou return

I am a paperboat
being tossed around
on the waves of the river

I do not know
Which way I would go
Where I will end up
Whether I will ever
Reach the shore

I might even turn turtle
And sink
In a blink

I am a slave

Of my mind
Which dictates

Of my faith
Which I follow blindly

Of my family
By bondage of affection

Of my profession
Which is all consuming

Of my ambitions
Which make me run like mad

On My 90th Birthday

All I wish now
is a shady nook
with a favourite book
and a lot of time for friends

A feeling of leisure
for my reading pleasure
that is how time be spent

An afternoon snooze
an evening of muse
a dash of booze
and, I have nothing more to choose.

Take any book
you cannot judge it
By its look

The cover is bright
Its contents often trite

Some books are
Like a smoke screen
You have to read
The lines in-between

There are books
Verbose and mere prattle
In your mind they would rattle

For certain books, there is a boom
Where the jackets
Match the decor
Of the drawing room

Then the books
Where the author himself →

Is on the center stage
His ego pops up at you
At very page

A book with your own frontispiece
With your name embossed in gold
Which looks so nice
You can have it all
For a price

At the going rate
Most of the books
Are not even worth
Their weight

Rarely, does a book
Comes your way
Which touches you
Makes you sit up and say—
Here is a book
Which I enjoyed reading
And
Would like to read again!

My beloved city is sick

My city
my beloved city
is seriously ill

Suffering from insomnia
she cannot go to sleep
even after midnight

Her heart is no longer
hale and hearty
the main arteries are choked

Her legs have started wobbling
the weight is too much to bear

She is getting hard of hearing
the din, the noises are deafening

Her vision is getting blurred
due to dust and dazzling lights

The only thing that
keeps her going
is her soul
which is still alive

She walked in
Thoroughly drenched
in the unexpected
winter rain
trembling like the
flickeringo flame of a candle

Her drenched body
filled up
my cold and bleak room
with a
certain intimate warmth

Child is the father of man
is a common saying
In the same strain

One may say

There is a MAN is every WOMAN
There is a grain of truth
in both aphorisms
The Child and the Woman
play a subtle role
in every man's life

Everything is growing at a fast pace
The rich are growing richer
The poor are becoming poorer
Population growing at a galloping pace
Pollution is simply choking
Corruption is rampant everywhere
Caste-vote-banks are swelling
Hindu-Muslim divide is widening alarmingly
It is growth all over
In our blessed country

Lahore

O, the days of yore
spent in my beloved Lahore

Lahore was a city slow in pace
But had its dignity and grace
And, in spite of its hustle and bustle
was seldom in a hurry or hassle

Almost every other day
friends would meet
to share latest gossip
and jokes not so discreet

Days at Lahore were
lazy and langourous
And nights
naughty and amorous

Lahore indeed had
a heart of gold
Eternally young
that would never grow old

My Epitaph

Here lies the man
who had only two passions
Muse and Music

His ambitions were small
His needs few
He was ever grateful
He got more than his due

He would often laugh and squirm
Whether or not
he was a book-worm

He was burried in books
all his life
So is he now
Amen!

❑ ❑ ❑

My Father, My Friend

(A poem by my son, Kapil)

He is 92 today
My father
The fine man who brought me
into this world

Today
Is his own day of birth
Every year we've celebrated this day
In this hurried, harried world
Not always successfully I admit
For ever so often
The ritual prayer-evening remained thus
Only ritual
Something to which we found
ourselves bound
My own heart
Inwardly oft would cry
Asking me

→

Why have you lost the meaning
The value of this day

I listened to my heart's enquiries
As one must
If one is not to be completely lost
By not talking even to one's own heart—
I had few answers
My father was lost to me
I knew
He was around, of course
But I felt him lost to me
And years went by

Often
I would think
Of those wondrous years of childhood
And of his shining, luminous face
Eyes alight
With excitement of things big
and small
Telling us tales
Inventive, unending tales
Inspiring tales
Tales of truth and goodness →

Of battle and honour
Above all, honour
That,
And idealism
He bequeathed
To my eager, accepting mind
As a young man
whenever I felt lost
Silently
I looked to him
to uphold truth and honour
Exactly as he had said
"Uphold these
Always
we must"
I held him to his word
In child-like trust
I knew I faltered aplenty
I wanted him never, ever to
And seethed inside
When he did too

And so I went away
In search of other Gods →

Who would never, ever fail
Just because I failed myself

In his eyes I would sometimes see
Hurt
He knew not why I was gone
He struggled for words
To ask me
I could have told him
But I didn't
I know not why
Cruel?
Unforgiving?
Arrogant?
Or,
Simply afraid?
In telling him
I would have to admit
First my failings to myself
And so the years just went by

And then one day
Poetry sprung forth from him
In a burst
Unending →

Irresistible
Unbounded
My father had set sail
To find himself anew
And all had changed
A man bravely
Face to face with himself
Accepting all
Good or bad
Weak and strong
Ideals burnished
Honour dusted-off
My father had found
courage
To be himself
To search for his truth

When he shyly showed me
what he wrote
I cried tears of joy
By now I knew too
It was not for anybody to forgive another
Each man must
Find his truth within himself →

Not for others
But
Above all
For himself

I marvelled
And I clapped
Thinking of a mentor
Who taught me things
When I thought I already knew it all
The mentor who always said
Be the best that you can be, that's all

Who am I ?
Truly?
My father wrote in a poem
And I rejoiced
He would find his answers
For now he spoke his heart
Meanwhile,
I had found a friend
My father, My friend